The Ultimate Kid's

Guide

to

FUN

Experiments, Projects, Games, and Fascinating Facts Every Kid Should Know

CAPSTONE PRESS
a capstone imprint

The Ultimate Kids'

Guide
to
FUN

Experiments, Projects, Games, and Fascinating Facts Every Kid Should Know

Make IT

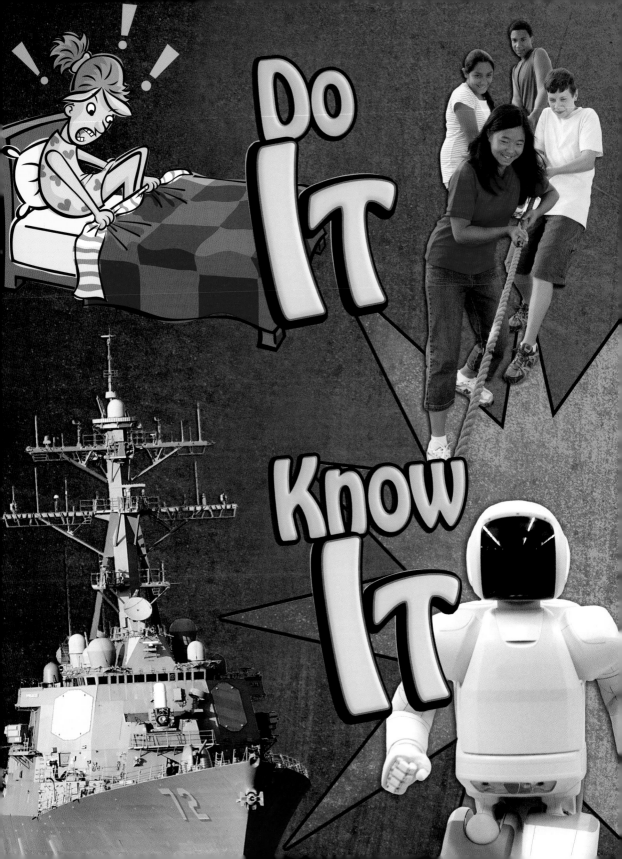

Table of Contents

Make It

BUILDING COOL STUFF 8

BUBBLING VOLCANO.................................. 10

FIZZLE ROCKS...................................... 12

VINEGAR LAUNCHER.................................. 14

BALLOON ROCKET.................................... 16

MILK CARTON BIRD FEEDER........................... 19

FLY HIGH KITE 22

WATER BRIDGE 24

PAPER BOAT 26

PAPER AIRPLANES 26

SONIC DART 28

RAPTOR 30

SUPER PLANE 32

BALLOON TWISTING 32

THE FLYING MOUSE 34

WALKING THE DOG 36

SWORD FIGHT! 40

Do It

CLASSIC GAMES... 40

BOX IT UP 42

PIPELINE.. 44

ROCK, PAPER, SCISSORS 46

ULTIMATE DISC TOSS 48

COIN COLLECTOR.................................... 49

PING-PONG SOCCER 50

TUG-OF-WAR 52

HORSE... 54

RINGER 57

PAPER FOOTBALL ....

PRANKS, TRICKS, AND PRACTICAL JOKES............ 60

DRIPPY 60

SAY CHEESE 61

LET 'ER RIP 62

BEACH BOMB 63

SHAKE, RATTLE, AND ROLL 64

YOU SNOOZE, YOU LOSE 66

LAUGHING THROUGH THE TEARS 68

PSST! HERE'S THE POOP! 70

GAG-O-BARF-O-RAMA 71

SCARED YA! 72

IT'S A GUSHER! 73

PEE YEEEWW! 74

SECRET LETTERS 75

IT'S ALL IN THE FOLD 76

DIVE-BOMBING EGG 78

JUMPING ACES 80

Know It

MILITARY VEHICLES 84

TANKS AND M VEHICLES 84

SHIPS 86

UNMANNED VEHICLES 88

ALIENS 90

TYPES OF ALIENS 90

MYSTERY IN ROSWELL 92

MONSTER TRUCKS 96

MONSTER TRUCK STANDOUTS 96

MONSTER CREATIONS 98

MUMMIES 100

ICE MUMMIES 100

BOG MUMMIES 102

MUMMIES AROUND THE WORLD 104

ROBOTS 106

ROBOT EXPLORERS 106

FUTURE ROBOTS 110

Make IT

What are you in the mood to make? Are you itching to build something with your very own hands? Well, look no further. Turn the pages to find projects you can put together. Have fun!

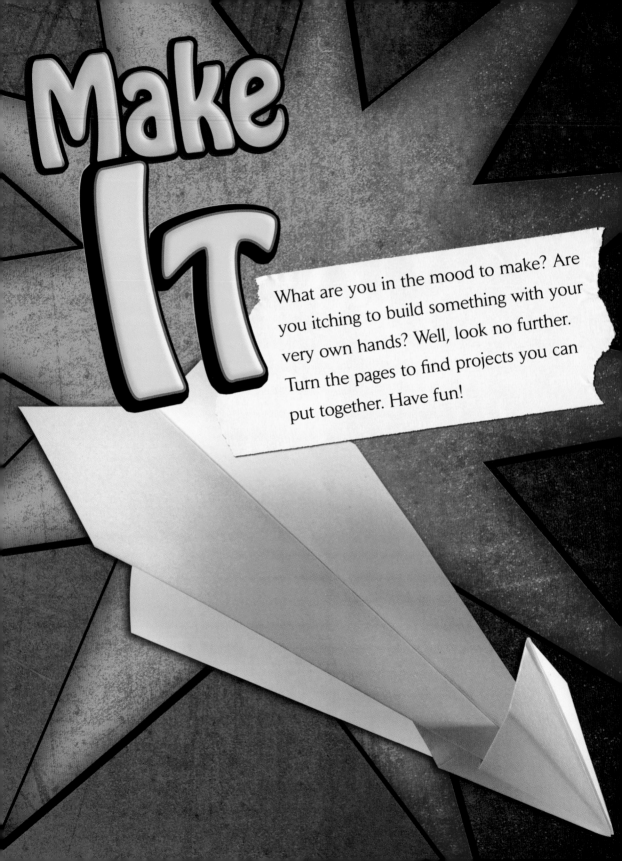

BUBBLING VOLCANO

What You Need

* tape
* paper snack cup
* paper plate
* aluminum foil
* scissors

* cookie sheet
  with raised lip
* 2 tablespoons (30 mL)
  of water

* red food coloring
* 1 tablespoon (15 mL)
  of baking soda
* 2 tablespoons (30 mL)
  of white vinegar

What's all that bubbling and frothing? It's just your very own erupting volcano! Build this, and your friends will be over in an instant to see all the action.

Step 1: Tape the bottom of the paper cup to the center of the paper plate.

Step 2: Cover the cup and plate with a long piece of foil. Make it long enough to fold around the edges of the plate.

Step 3: Use scissors to poke a hole in the foil where it covers the center of the cup. Cut four slits from the hole to the edges of the cup to create tabs. Fold the tabs down and tape them inside the cup.

Step 4: Set your volcano on a large cookie sheet. Pour the water into the cone of the volcano. Then add several drops of red food coloring and the baking soda.

Step 5: Pour in the vinegar and watch your volcano erupt!

Note: The volcano erupts because the vinegar and the baking soda have a chemical reaction. The vinegar is an acid that reacts with the baking soda to make a froth.

FIZZLE ROCKS

What You Need

* spoon
* 1/4 cup (60 mL) of water
* 1 cup (240 mL) of baking soda
* food coloring
* small mixing bowl
* small plastic toys
* plate
* 4 cups (960 mL) of white vinegar
* large, clear bowl

Can rocks dissolve? These rocks do. And your friends will think the prizes hidden inside them are super cool!

Step 1: Use a spoon to mix the water, baking soda, and a couple drops of food coloring together in the mixing bowl. A stiff dough should form. If it seems too wet, add more baking soda. If it seems too dry, add more water.

Step 2: Scoop a spoonful of the dough into the palm of your hand. Press one of your prizes into the dough. Roll the dough around in your hands until it looks like a rock. Be sure to use enough dough to hide the prize.

Step 3: Place each finished rock on the plate. Put the plate in a safe place overnight so the rocks have time to dry and harden.

Step 4: When you're ready to surprise your friends, pour the vinegar into the clear bowl. Then gently drop one of your rocks into the vinegar.

Step 5: Watch your friends stare in amazement as the dough fizzles away to nothing. All that's left behind are the hidden prizes!

VINEGAR LAUNCHER

What You Need

* cork
* plastic soda bottle
* tape
* paper towel

* 1 teaspoon (5 mL) of baking soda
* toilet paper
* funnel

* white vinegar
* water
* safety glasses

What can you make with a soda bottle and a couple of ordinary baking ingredients? A really cool rocket! With a good, hard shake, your rocket will head for the sky!

Step 1: Bring all of your items to a safe outdoor area away from people. Make sure the cork fits snugly into the neck of the bottle. If it doesn't, wrap tape around the cork until it does.

Step 2: Rip the paper towel into 1-inch strips. Tape the strips to the top of the cork. These strips will help you see the cork when it launches.

Step 3: Pour the baking soda into the center of one square of toilet paper. Then carefully fold the square so that you have a tidy little packet. Set aside.

Step 4: Place the funnel in the neck of the bottle. Pour about a half-inch of vinegar into the bottle. Then pour in enough water to fill the bottle about half full.

Step 5: Put on your safety glasses. Carefully point the bottle away from you and your friends. Drop the baking soda packet into the bottle. Then firmly wedge the cork into the bottle. Give the bottle a hard shake. Quickly place the bottle on the ground and stand back.

Whooooosh! Watch your cork rocket blast into the air.

BALLOON ROCKET

What You Need

* 15-foot piece of fishing line
* plastic drinking straw
* 2 sturdy chairs
* hot dog-shaped balloon
* tape

Balloons aren't just for birthday parties. They can be rockets in disguise. Build a zip line and get ready to blast off!

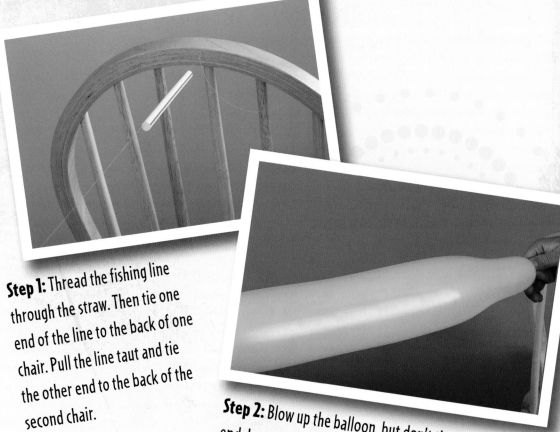

Step 1: Thread the fishing line through the straw. Then tie one end of the line to the back of one chair. Pull the line taut and tie the other end to the back of the second chair.

Step 2: Blow up the balloon, but don't tie the end. Instead, pinch or twist the end to keep the air from escaping.

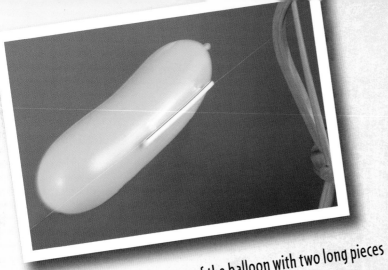

Metric Conversions	
1 inch	2.5 centimeters
1.5 inch	4 cm
10 inch	25 cm
12 inch	30 cm
5 feet	1.5 meters

Step 3: Tape the straw to the top of the balloon with two long pieces of tape. Make sure the closed end of the balloon is facing a chair.

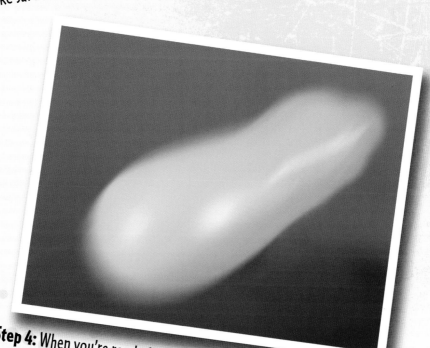

Step 4: When you're ready for your rocket to blast off, let go of the pinched end of the balloon. It will zoom down the fishing line on your air power!

MILK CARTON BIRD FEEDER

What You Need

* stapler
* empty half-gallon (1.9-liter) cardboard milk carton
* hole punch
* ruler
* pencil

* utility knife
* 12-inch wooden dowel
* brown or green nontoxic poster paint
* paintbrush

* wooden craft sticks
* hot glue gun
* twine
* birdseed

Are you looking for a recycling project to help the planet? Here's one that will make the birds in your neighborhood very happy.

Step 1: Staple the opened lip of the milk carton shut. Then use a hole punch to make a hole in the center of the carton's top edge. You will hang the bird feeder from this hole.

Step 2: Lay the carton on its side. Measure 5 inches from the top of the carton and mark this spot with a pencil. Then measure 8 inches from the top of the carton and mark this spot too. Have an adult use the utility knife to cut a square between the two lines. Leave about a half-inch on the left and right edges of the cut.

Step 3: Turn the carton over and repeat Step 2. You now have openings on two sides for birds to use.

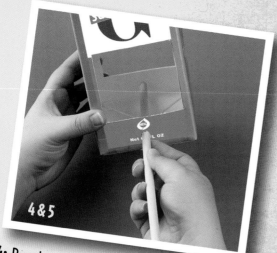

Step 4: Punch a hole about 1 inch below the square opening with the hole punch. Slide the wooden dowel through the hole until it butts up against the other side of the carton. Mark an "X" where you feel it hitting the carton. Punch a second hole here.

Step 5: Slide the wooden dowel through both holes. The dowel should stick out evenly on both sides. Birds now have a perch to rest on while they're eating.

Step 6: Paint the outside of the carton to decorate it.

PROJECT CONTINUED
ON PAGE 18 ▶▶▶

7 & 8

Step 7: Attach the craft sticks to the top of the feeder with the hot glue gun. Paint the roof green.

Step 8: Loop twine through the hole you made in the top of the feeder.

TIP: YOU CAN MAKE BIRD FEEDERS FOR SMALLER BIRDS BY USING THE MILK CARTONS YOU GET AT SCHOOL.

Pour birdseed into the bird feeder. Hang it in a tree and your birdy café is open for business!

FLY HIGH KITE

What You Need

- 24-inch wood dowel
- 20-inch wood dowel
- utility knife
- tape measure

- pencil
- kite string
- scissors
- heavy-duty plastic trash bag

- packing tape
- large sewing needle
- twine
- ribbon

Are you looking for a windy day activity? Make a kite. Ben Franklin did it and so can you.

Step 2: On the longer dowel, use your tape measure and pencil to mark a line that is 6 inches from one end. On the shorter dowel, mark a line that is 10 inches from the end.

Step 1: Ask an adult to cut a notch in each end of the dowels with a utility knife.

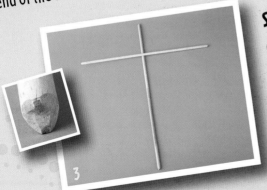

Step 3: Place the short dowel on top of the long dowel so the marks from step 2 cross. Make sure all the notches in the tips are parallel with the table.

PROJECT CONTINUED ON PAGE 20 ▶▶▶

19

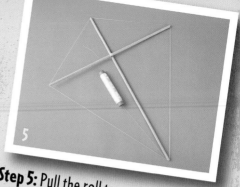

Step 4: Wind the kite string around the dowels where they cross. As you wind the string, make an "X" pattern around the sticks until they are bound tightly together. Make sure the notches stay parallel to the table. Leave about 5 inches of the string hanging freely.

Step 5: Pull the roll toward the end of one of the dowels. Thread the string through the notch in the dowel. Then continue winding the string through the other three notches. Wind the string around the outside of the kite one more time. Make sure the string is tight.

Step 6: Pull the string to the center of the kite and wrap it around the X a few more times. Then cut the string off the roll, leaving about 5 inches free. Tie this end tightly to the other free end from step 4.

Step 7: Place the kite frame on top of the trash bag. Cut the bag around the kite, leaving several inches on all sides. Fold these edges over the sides of the kite frame and tape them down. Add more tape to the top and bottom tips of your kite to strengthen these areas.

Step 8: Cut a 2-foot piece of string. Use the sewing needle to thread the string through the plastic and around the dowels at the top and bottom tips of the kite. Tie the ends of the string together. This string is called a bridle.

Step 9: Tie your kite string about one-third of the way down the bridle. You can move the knot higher or lower later if the kite has trouble flying.

Step 10: For the tail, tape a 6-foot piece of twine to the bottom point of your kite. Then tie ribbon down the length of the twine to give your kite extra stability.

Fly your kite on a breezy day in an open field or park.

WATER BRIDGE

What You Need

* large liquid measuring cup
* water
* blue food coloring
* 2-foot piece of rope
* bowl
* tape

Here's a challenge for you. Try building a rope bridge that allows water to flow from a measuring cup to a bowl. Even better, challenge a friend to see who can finish the project first.

Step 1: Find a spot outside. Fill the measuring cup with water. Add a few drops of food coloring. Then dunk the rope in the measuring cup to get it wet.

Step 2: Place the bowl on the ground. Tape the bottom end of the rope inside the bowl. Place the other end of the rope across the measuring cup and over the spout. Hold the end of the rope with your thumb.

Step 3: Hold the measuring cup up in the air, away from the bowl, until the rope between them is taut. The rope will be at an angle, as shown.

> TIP: IF YOU SET UP TWO WATER BRIDGES, YOU AND A FRIEND CAN RACE TO SEE WHO CAN GET THE MOST WATER INTO THE BOWL THE FASTEST.

Slowly tip the measuring cup so the water in the cup begins to trickle down the rope. When you get the hang of it, the water from the measuring cup will end up in the bowl. Until then, expect to get a bit wet!

Paper Boat

Got water? Then you need a boat! Fortunately, with just a page of newspaper, you can quickly make your own. Happy sailing, mate!

What You Need

* double-spread newspaper page

Step 1: Rip the newspaper page in two down the long middle seam.

Step 2: Fold the paper in half.

Step 3: Fold the paper in half again and unfold.

Step 4: Fold the top corners to the center crease.

Step 5: Fold the top layer of the bottom edge.

Step 6: Fold the corners behind the model and turn the model over.

Step 7: Fold the bottom edge as you did in step 5.

Step 8: Slide your thumbs into the model and pull the triangle open. Press the model into a diamond shape.

Step 9: Fold the top layer to the point and turn the model over.

Step 10: Fold the remaining layer to the point.

Step 11: Open and press the model into a diamond shape as you did in step 8.

Step 12: Pull the two points apart. Spread apart the bottom of the model to help the boat stay open.

Your boat is now ready to sail!

SONIC DART

What You Need

★ 8.5- by 11-inch paper

The sonic dart gives the classic paper airplane model some style. With sleek lines and raised wing flaps, this plane looks supersonic with a gentle throw.

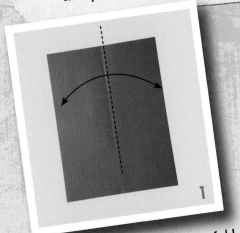

Step 1: Valley fold edge to edge and unfold.

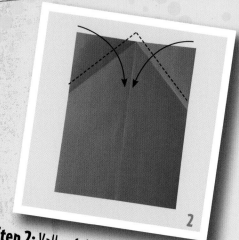

Step 2: Valley fold the corners to the center.

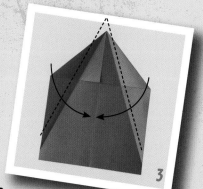

Step 3: Valley fold the edges to the center.

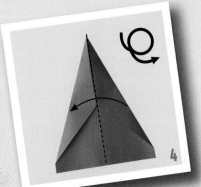

Step 4: Valley fold the model in half and rotate.

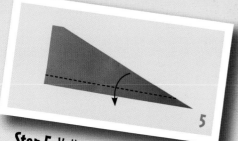

Step 5: Valley fold the top layer so the body of the plane is about 1 inch deep. Repeat behind.

Step 6: Valley fold the edge of the wing. Repeat behind.

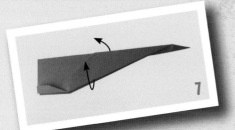

Step 7: Lift the wings.

Step 8: Lift the wing flaps so they stand up at 90-degree angles.

Your finished sonic dart is ready to toss.

How to make a valley fold: Crease the paper along the dashed lines and fold the top surface of the paper against itself like a book.

RAPTOR

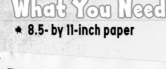

Depending on your throw, the raptor can be a glider or a stunt plane. Luckily the plane's sturdy construction handles repeated flights like a pro.

Step 1: Valley fold edge to edge and unfold.

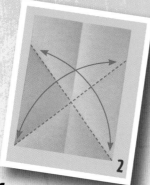

Step 2: Valley fold in both directions and unfold.

Step 3: Turn the paper over.

Step 4: Valley fold so the corners meet at A and unfold.

Step 5: Turn the paper over.

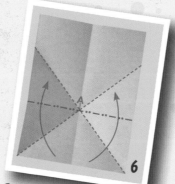

Step 6: Push at point A. Collapse the paper on the existing creases to form a triangle.

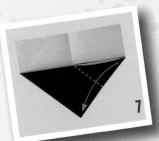

Step 7: Valley fold the top layer to the point.

Step 8: Valley fold to the center and unfold.

Step 9: Valley fold to the center and unfold.

Step 10: Rabbit ear fold on the crease formed in steps 8 and 9.

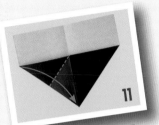

Step 11: Repeat steps 7 through 10 on the left side.

Step 12: Mountain fold the point.

Step 13: Valley fold the model in half and rotate.

Step 14: Valley fold the top layer. Repeat behind.

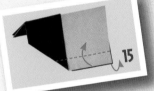

Step 15: Valley fold the top layer. Repeat behind.

Step 16: Lift the wings.

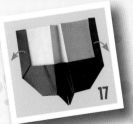

Step 17: Lift the wing flaps so they stand up at 90-degree angles.

Your finished raptor is ready to go.

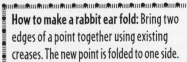

How to make a rabbit ear fold: Bring two edges of a point together using existing creases. The new point is folded to one side.

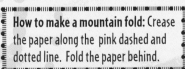

How to make a mountain fold: Crease the paper along the pink dashed and dotted line. Fold the paper behind.

29

SUPER PLANE

What You Need

* 8.5- by 11-inch paper

If your school has a paper airplane contest, learn to fold the super plane. It is great for distance. This incredible plane can easily fly distances of more than 45 feet.

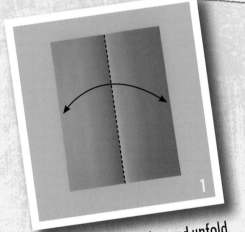

Step 1: Valley fold edge to edge and unfold.

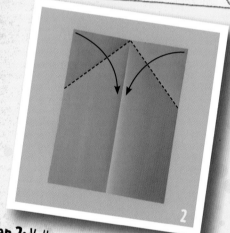

Step 2: Valley fold the corners to the center.

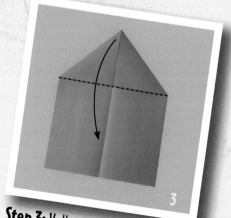

Step 3: Valley fold the point.

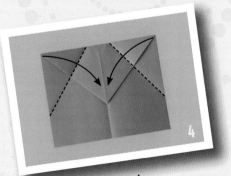

Step 4: Valley fold the corners to the center.

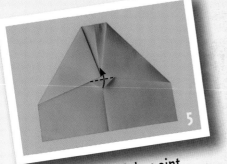

Step 5: Valley fold the point.

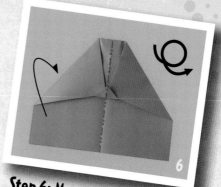

Step 6: Mountain fold the model in half and rotate.

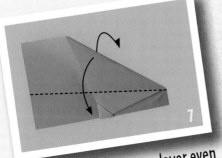

Step 7: Valley fold the top layer even with the bottom edge. Repeat behind.

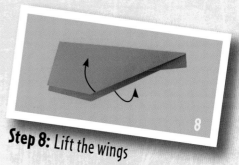

Step 8: Lift the wings

Your super plane is ready to throw.

THE FLYING MOUSE

What You Need

★ one white, gray, or pink 260 balloon

Have you ever seen a mouse fly? You're about to! Make these balloons for your friends and see whose mouse can fly the highest.

1 Inflate a 260 balloon to 10-12 inches. This balloon will have a very long tail. Do not burp it. This will make it fly better.

2 Starting at the nozzle end, twist a 1.5-inch head bubble.

3 Hold the first bubble, and twist a 1-inch bubble to make the first ear.

A 260 is a balloon that inflates to 2 inches in diameter and 60 inches long.

4 Grab the ear bubble in the middle and pull it slightly out.

5 Twist the two ends of the ear bubble together. Steps 4 and 5 are called the ear twist.

6 Repeat steps 3 through 5 to create the second ear.

I'll bet you didn't know you could burp a balloon! Burping means letting a small puff of air out of your balloon. This slightly softens the balloon and makes it easier to tie and twist. Unless you're instructed not to, you should always burp a balloon after inflating it. Tie the balloon closed, and you're ready to twist.

7 Draw a cute face on the first bubble to complete your mouse.

TO MAKE YOUR MOUSE FLY:

1 Make the "OK" sign with your thumb and pointer finger.

2 Rest the mouse on your hand. Dangle the tail through the loop of your thumb and finger.

4

3 Grab the tail with your other hand and stretch it back as far as you can.

Release the tail and watch your mouse soar!

WALK THE DOG

What You Need

* one 260 balloon of any color

Now for the classic—the balloon dog. This is the basic balloon animal shape. Once you learn this, you will be able to make a horse, giraffe, squirrel, and more!

1 Inflate a 260 balloon. Leave a 6-inch tail.

Use a hand-held balloon pump to inflate balloons. Using your mouth to inflate lots of balloons is bad for your lungs.

2 Starting at the nozzle end, twist a 2-inch bubble for the nose.

3 Keep holding the 2-inch bubble, and twist two 1.5-inch bubbles for ears. Now you have a string of three bubbles.

4 Hold the ears side-by-side and twist them together. This is called the bubble twist. It locks the ears in place.

5

Twist a 1-inch neck bubble and two 3-inch front leg bubbles.

6

Hold the legs together and do another bubble twist to lock them together.

7

Twist a 2-inch body bubble and two 2-inch leg bubbles.

8

Use another bubble twist to lock the leg bubbles together. The remaining balloon is the tail.

How to hold and twist:

Grip balloons firmly. You need one hand on either side of the spot where the twist will appear. Gently squish the balloon with your fingers and thumbs to make it easier to twist. Then twist one hand away from you for five to eight full rotations. Doing several rotations keeps the twist secure.

Sword Fight!

What You Need

* a 260 balloon of any color

Do you want to have a sword fight with a friend? This is a great way to do it without getting hurt. The simple sword can be made with just three twists. The knight sword requires a bit more skill.

The Simple Sword

1 Inflate a 260 balloon, leaving a 0.5-inch tail.

2 Twist a 1-inch bubble at the nozzle end of the balloon.

3 Next to the 1-inch bubble, twist a 4-inch bubble.

4 Loop twist the 4-inch bubble.

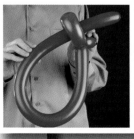

5 Pass the front end of the balloon through the loop. Pull until you make a handle.

The Knight Sword

1 Inflate a 260, leaving a 1-inch tail.

2 Twist a 4-inch bubble at the nozzle end of the balloon.

3 Twist another 4-inch bubble, and loop twist it.

5 Twist two 1-inch ear twists. Place them between the loop twists.

4 Make another 4-inch loop twist.

How to make a loop twist: To create a large loop, twist the head and body sections together.

DO IT

Admit it. You love to play games. And you love to play tricks on your friends and family. You have definitely come to the right place! Take a look at the classic games and tricks, and get moving!

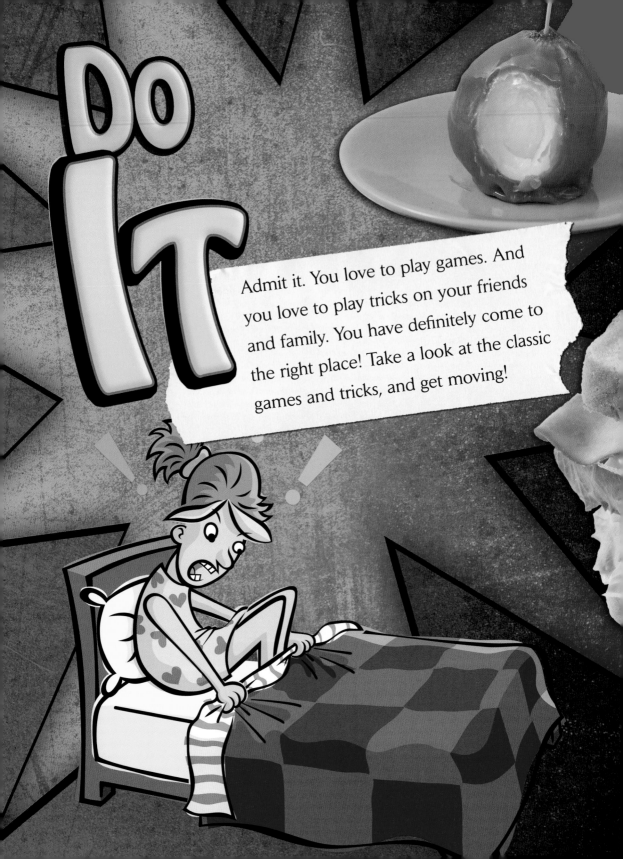

BOX IT UP

What You Need

* pencils
* paper
* 2 players

Your grandparents probably played this old paper and pencil game. If they're not around to play, grab a friend. The player who forms the most boxes by connecting the dots wins!

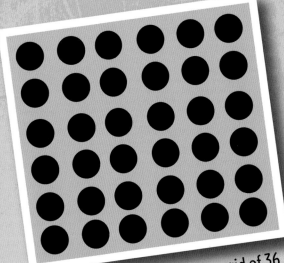

Step 1: Use a pencil to draw a grid of 36 small dots on your paper, as shown.

Step 2: Ask your opponent to draw a line between two dots. This line can be horizontal or vertical.

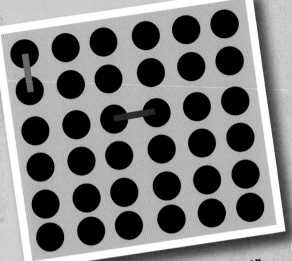

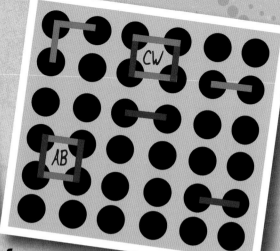

Step 3: Now draw your own line between two dots. Continue taking turns.

Step 4: At first you'll be able to draw lines far from your opponent's. But soon the lines will begin forming boxes. When your opponent draws the third line of a box, your goal is to add the fourth line to complete it. Your opponent has the same goal.

Step 5: Put your initials in each box you complete. Your opponent should do the same.

Step 6: Each time you complete a box, you take another turn. Your turn ends only when your last line doesn't complete a box.

Step 7: When all the dots are connected, count the number of boxes each player claimed. The player with the most boxes wins.

PIPELINE

What You Need

- ★ pencil
- ★ paper
- ★ red marker
- ★ blue marker
- ★ 2 players

Like Box It Up, this paper and pencil game uses dots. But this game is a lot harder. To win, a player has to draw one long line all the way across the board.

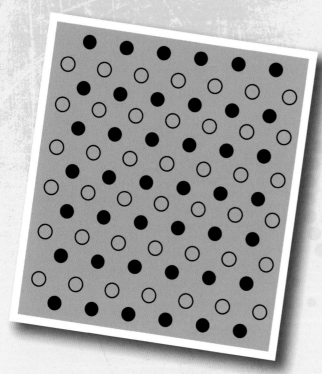

Step 1: Use a pencil to draw 13 horizontal rows of dots and circles on your paper, as shown.

Step 2: Let your opponent choose either the dots or the circles. If she chooses circles, she may only connect the circles. Then you may only connect the dots.

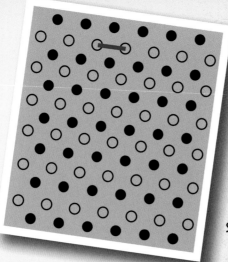

Step 3: Let your opponent choose a marker. She starts the game by drawing a line between two of her circles. The line can be horizontal or vertical. Her goal is to win by drawing a continuous line across her seven rows. Your goal is to draw a continuous line across your seven rows.

Step 4: On your turn, use your marker to draw a line. You can begin far from your opponent's line. Or you can block her line by drawing a line in front of hers. Players may not draw a line through another line.

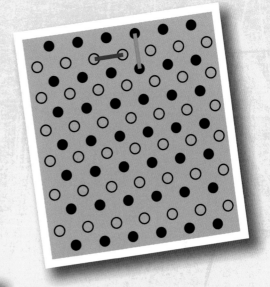

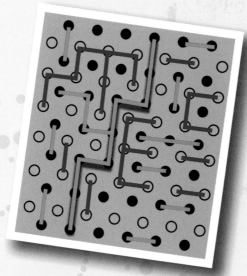

Step 5: If you blocked her, she must start a new line on her turn. If you didn't block her line, she could decide to block yours. The winner is the first person to draw a continuous line across seven rows.

43

ROCK, PAPER, SCISSORS

What You Need

* 2 players

This game is as "old as the hills," which means it's been around forever! It remains popular because you only use your hands. It can be played anytime, anywhere.

Step 1: Show the other player the game's three hand gestures. They are:

Paper: Hold your hand out flat with your palm down.

Rock: Make your hand into a fist.

Scissors: Make a fist, but extend your first and second fingers out in a "V" shape.

Step 2: Make sure the players agree on the rules. Rock wins over scissors because rock smashes scissors. Scissors wins over paper because a scissors cuts paper. Paper wins over rock because paper wraps around rock.

Step 3: Players start the game by tapping their fists three times on their open palms. On the third tap, each player gestures with rock, paper, or scissors.

Step 4: If the gestures are different, determine who wins based on the rules above. If the players pick the same gesture, it's a tie.

Step 5: The winner is the player who leads after 10 rounds.

ULTIMATE DISC TOSS

What You Need

* large rectangular grassy area
* 4 plastic cones
* coin

* flying disc
* 8 to 14 players

Who knew a spinning plastic disc would create so many die-hard game fans? Here's your chance to join them on the field.

Step 1: Divide the players into two teams. Give each team two cones to mark the end zones and sidelines. Each end zone should be about 100 feet wide. The two end zones should be about 200 feet apart.

Step 2: Toss a coin to determine the offensive team. These players have control of the disc first.

Step 3: Both teams line up in their end zones. Play begins when a defensive player throws the disc toward the offensive team. The offensive team tries to catch the disc before it hits the ground. When players do, the offensive team runs toward the defensive team's end zone. They toss the disc between one another as they run down the field.

Step 4: As in football, the defensive players shadow offensive players. The defensive players try to grab the disc or knock it to the ground before it reaches their end zone. However, players cannot touch each other. Shoving, kicking, and tackling are not allowed.

Step 5: The offensive team continues moving the disc up the field by throwing it in any direction to one another. Any player holding the disc must stop and throw the disc within 10 seconds.

Step 6: If the disc hits the ground while being passed, the defensive team gains control of the disc. This is called a turnover. Turnovers also occur when a defensive player catches the disc or the disc goes out of bounds. Turnovers do not stop play. The defensive team becomes the offense if it takes control of the disc. That team then tries to move the disc to its opponent's end zone.

Step 7: When players catch the disc in their opponent's end zone, they score a point.

Step 8: After a score, the scoring team restarts play the same way the game started in step 3.

Step 9: Each team may call four time-outs, two per each half of the game. If the final score is to be nine points, then the halftime break occurs when a team scores five points.

Step 10: Play continues until an agreed-upon score is reached.

COIN COLLECTOR

* **4 or more players**   * **blindfold for each player**   * **15 assorted coins for each player**

Step 1: Choose someone to be the judge.

Is it possible to correctly sort coins into piles if you can't use your eyes? Slip on a blindfold and see how you do. Your fingers will have to work overtime as they try to "see" the coins.

Step 2: The judge sits the players in a line. Then he makes sure they put their blindfolds on correctly. When satisfied, he tells the players to put their hands on their laps.

Step 3: The judge puts 15 coins in front of each player. Then the judge yells, "Go!"

Step 4: The players rush to sort the coins into piles by denomination. Will they be able to tell a penny from a nickel? If you want to make the game harder, have the players also organize their piles in order from the largest value to the smallest value. Or add in some rarely used coins, such as half dollars and dollars.

Step 5: When a player thinks he has his piles sorted correctly, he yells, "Stop!"

Step 6: The other players immediately put their hands on their laps. If the judge decides the piles are right, the player wins and the game ends. But if he's sorted them wrong, he's disqualified and the judge restarts the game.

PING-PONG SOCCER

What You Need

* coffee table
* Ping-Pong ball
* 4 players

Some of your friends probably like to boast about their skills on the playing field. Have them try this game. They might get really winded!

Step 1: Have the players divide into two teams. The teams should kneel at opposite ends of the coffee table.

Step 2: Play begins with one player dropping the Ping-Pong ball in the center of the table.

Step 3: Each team tries to blow the ball off the opposing team's end of the table. Doing so earns the successful team a point!

Step 4: If the ball rolls off the sides of the table, neither team scores. Continue the game by repeating step 2.

Step 5: Play continues until a set score is reached.

TUG-OF-WAR

What You Need

* large outdoor area
* electrical tape
* thick hemp rope, 100 feet in length
* tape measure
* 8 players
* 1 judge

Sometimes you need to know if your friends can pull together in a tough situation. In this game you'll need some friends with real muscle!

Step 1: Find a big grassy area, such as your backyard or a park. There should be enough space to pull the ends of the rope tight.

Step 2: Lay a long strip of electrical tape on the grass. The teams will stand on opposite sides of this dividing line.

Step 3: Unwind the rope. Mark the center of the rope by wrapping a short piece of electrical tape around it.

Step 4: Use a tape measure to measure 5 feet to the right of the center point. Mark this spot with a long piece of the tape. The tape should hang down about 1 foot from the rope. This tape is one team's flag.

Step 5: Measure 5 feet to the left of the center point. Mark the rope as you did in step 4.

Step 6: Measure another 2 feet from each of the marks made in steps 4 and 5. Mark the spots by wrapping short pieces of tape around the rope. These lines mark how closely the teams can stand to the center of the rope.

Step 7: Divide the players into two teams. Have the teams grasp opposite ends of the rope. Stagger the members on each team so that there are members on the left and right sides of the rope. This will keep them from tripping over one another.

Step 8: Be sure the two heaviest players are last in line.

Step 9: To start the game, position the center of the rope directly over the dividing line on the grass.

Step 10: When the judge yells "Go!," the two teams pull as hard as they can. The goal is to pull the other team's flag over the dividing line.

HORSE

What You Need

* basketball
* basketball hoop

* 2 or more players

This basketball game gives you the chance to show off your awesome shooting skills. Just don't spell the word "horse."

Step 1: Grab your basketball and head for a nearby basketball hoop.

Step 2: The game starts with the first player shooting the ball from any position he chooses. If he makes a basket, the second player must copy the shot from the same spot on the court. If the second player misses the shot, she gets the "h" from the word "horse."

Step 3: If the first player misses, the second player can shoot from any spot on the court. If her shot makes the basket, the first player must copy it.

Step 4: Play continues like this until one player gets all the letters in the word "horse" and loses the game.

Step 5: For three or more players, each player gets a chance to copy the first player's shot. Anyone who misses the shot gets a letter. Then the second player throws a new shot that must be copied by the other players.

Step 6: Play then cycles through all the players, with each getting a chance to make the new shot.

Step 7: The first player to spell "horse" is out. Play continues until there is only one player left. That player wins the game.

RINGER

What You Need

* chalk
* smooth play surface
* 1 glass shooter marble per player
* 13 glass marbles
* 2 to 6 players

Marble games are great fun. They were even played by ancient Egyptians. For most people the fun comes from the satisfying sound they hear when an opponent's orb is knocked out of play!

Step 1: Use the chalk to draw a 10-foot diameter circle on the ground.

Step 2: Allow the players some warm-up time. If any are new to shooting a marble, teach them how with these steps:

A. Hold out the hand you write with.

B. Tuck your thumb into your palm.

C. Make a fist, wrapping your fingers around your thumb. Keep your thumb knuckle level with your index finger.

D. Grip the marble between the tip of your index finger and your thumb knuckle.

E. To shoot, flick your thumb hard against the marble. Keep the rest of your hand in a fist.

Step 3: When ready to play, arrange the 13 marbles in a cross in the center of the ring. The easiest way to make the cross is to put one marble in the center. Then add three marbles facing east, west, north, and south.

Step 4: Players take turns using their shooter marble to knock any marbles out of the ring. A player's first shot can be anywhere on the edge of the circle. If a player's shooter does not travel more than 10 inches, the player may call out "Slips!" and shoot again from the same spot.

GAME CONTINUED
ON PAGE 56 ▶▶▶

Step 5: If a player knocks a marble outside the ring, she gets to keep it. She then gets another turn.

Step 6: If a player's shooter marble is still inside the circle for her second shot, she may place her nonshooting hand inside the circle. That way she can balance herself on her knuckles. If she steps into the ring, she gives up a marble. Her turn ends if she misses a marble. Her turn also ends if her shooter rolls out of the circle or a marble she hits fails to roll out of the circle.

Step 7: If the player's first shot doesn't knock a marble out, her turn ends. If her shooter is still in the ring, she must leave it there until the other players have taken a turn. The other players will likely try to shoot at it. Why? Because a player gets a second shot if she hits another player's shooter marble. In addition, if a player's shooter gets knocked out, she's out of the game. Any marbles she has collected go to the player who knocked her shooter out of the circle.

Step 8: If a player's shooter is still in the circle on her next turn, she resumes play with it, as she did in step 6. She must not step into the circle but can balance herself on her knuckles. If her shooter is outside the circle, she shoots from the edge of the circle.

Step 9: The game ends when the last marble is shot out of the circle. The player with the most marbles wins the game.

PAPER FOOTBALL

What You Need

* notebook paper
* scissors
* rectangular table
* coin
* 2 players

Think you have a steady hand and a sharp eye? Then prove it with this paper version of football!

Step 1: Cut your piece of paper in half lengthwise.

Step 2: Fold the paper over in half.

Step 3: Fold the lower right edge up to the fold edge.

Step 4: Fold the triangle until you're left with a rectangle at the end of the paper.

Step 5: Fold the top left corner of the rectangle down.

Step 6: Tuck the flap into the pocket of the triangle.

GAME CONTINUED ON PAGE 58 ▶▶▶

Step 7: Opponents sit on opposite sides of a table. They flip a coin to see who will go first. The winner is the "kicker." The loser is the "receiver."

Step 8: The game starts with the kicker resting the football over the edge of the table. He flicks the football with his index finger. His goal is to launch the football and land it close to his opponent's edge of the table. Wherever the football lands is where the receiver begins play. If the ball flies off the table, the receiver places the football in the center of the table. He starts play from there.

Step 9: The players then take turns flicking the football back and forth across the table. When a player gets the football to hang over his opponent's edge of the table, he scores a touchdown. Touchdowns are worth six points.

Step 10: After scoring a touchdown, the player may try for a two-point conversion. He places the football in the center of the table. He then flicks the ball. If the football hangs over his opponent's edge of the table, he gets two points.

Step 11: After a touchdown a player may try for an extra point instead of a two-point conversion. An extra point is earned by kicking the football through two goalposts. The opposing player makes the goalposts with his fingers.

Step 12: After a two-point conversion or an extra point attempt, the opposing player kicks off and regular play resumes.

Step 13: If the football flies off the table during regular play, it is out of bounds. The football goes to the opposing player for a kickoff. If either player gets three out of bounds, his opponent can try a field goal. Field goals are kicked the same way as extra points, but they are worth three points.

Step 14: The game is played for an agreed amount of time. When time runs out, the player with the highest score wins.

DRIPPY

This easy prank will leave your victims all wet. They'll never suspect a thing when you hand them what looks like a normal cup.

What You Need

* sewing needle
* plastic cup
* water

Step 1: Use a sewing needle to poke several holes in the middle of the cup. Store the cup in a safe place until a friend says she's "dying of thirst."

Step 2: When you hear those magic words, jump up and smile sweetly. Then offer to get her a cool drink.

Step 3: As you fill the cup, cover the holes with your thumb so the water doesn't pour out. Then hand over the cup with the holes facing your victim. She will think you're being nice – until she drinks from the cup and water dribbles down her shirt!

TIP: THE TIME TO SLINK AWAY IS WHEN SHE TIPS THE CUP.

SAY CHEESE

What You Need

* ★ sliced bread
* ★ individual cheese slices wrapped in plastic

Nearly everyone likes a cheese sandwich. But no one will like this recipe!

Step 1: Offer to make your victim a cheese sandwich.

Step 2: Make the sandwich, but "forget" to remove the plastic wrapping on the cheese.

Step 3: Hand your victim the sandwich. Then get ready to apologize after he bites down on the plastic.

TIP: THIS PRANK WORKS BEST WITH VICTIMS ON WHOM YOU'VE NEVER PLAYED FOOD TRICKS.

LET 'ER RIP

If there's one practical joke that's perfect for a public place, this is it. Why? Because you want your victim surrounded by others when you let 'er rip!

Step 1: Rip the rag into long strips. Each strip should be about 2 inches wide.

Step 2: Start a new rip in each strip that is about 2 inches long.

Step 3: Hide the strips in your pocket until you're ready to pull the prank.

RRRRIIPP

Step 4: "Accidentally" bump an item belonging to one of your friends onto the ground. Have one of your strips ready.

Step 5: When your friend bends down to pick it up, rip the strip in half.

Expect to hear lots of laughs as your victim reaches back to feel if his pants are ripped!

BEACH BOMB

What You Need

* beach towels
* sandy beach
* sand shovel

Nothing's quite as fun as a day at the beach. And with this prank, the fun will double. That's because with just a bit of muscle power, your victim will sink to a new low!

Step 1: Lay your towel out on the beach, close to your friend's towel. Keep your sand shovel hidden.

Step 2: When your friend leaves for the snack shop, pull back his towel. Quickly dig a hole in the center. The deeper you dig the hole, the better. Cover the hole by spreading the towel back over it.

Step 3: Act completely surprised when your friend sinks into the hole when he returns. Blame the hole on sand crabs!

SHAKE, RATTLE, AND ROLL

What You Need

* ★ letter-size envelope
* ★ marker
* ★ wire coat hanger
* ★ wire cutters
* ★ rubber band
* ★ large coat button

Do you have friends who are squeamish about snakes? This prank is perfect for them. But be warned, some of your pals might scream. Don't stand too close!

Step 1: On the outside of the envelope, write "Rattlesnake Eggs. Handle with Care."

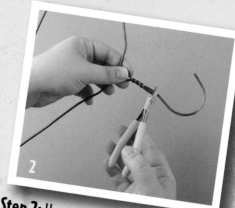

Step 2: Use wire cutters to snip the curved hook off of the coat hanger.

Step 3: Slip the rubber band through two holes of the button. Loop the ends of the rubber band over the ends of the U-shaped wire that you cut in step 2.

Step 4: Wind the button until the rubber band is twisted tightly. Place the button inside the envelope. Grasp the button through the envelope with your other hand to keep it wound up.

RRAAAAATTLE

RATTLESNAKE EGGS

Step 5: Invite your friends to view the rattlesnake eggs you're babysitting until they hatch. When they gather around, open the envelope so they can peek inside. Then let go of the button and watch them jump. They'll think your noisy little snakes have hatched and are about to strike!

TIP: DON'T LET YOUR FRIENDS SEE INSIDE THE ENVELOPE BEFORE THE RATTLING BEGINS.

YOU SNOOZE, YOU LOSE

What You Need

* a bed with top and bottom sheets of the same color or pattern

One sneaky way to get back at brothers and sisters is to short-sheet their beds. You'll need about 5 minutes in their bedrooms, so wait until they're taking a shower!

Step 1: Carefully study how the bed looks before you touch it. You must make sure it looks exactly the same when you're finished.

Step 2: Remove the top sheet and any blankets. Leave the bottom sheet on the mattress.

Step 3: Spread the top sheet out over the bottom sheet. Then tuck the top sheet under the mattress at the head of the bed instead of the foot of the bed.

Step 4: Grab the loose edge of the top sheet at the foot of the bed. Fold it up toward the head of the bed. You've just created a U-shaped sack.

Step 5: Cover the sheet with the blankets, pillows, and other items that were on the bed before you started. Then split so you don't get caught. You'll know by the shouts that your prank was successful!

LAUGHING THROUGH THE TEARS

What You Need

* wax paper
* cookie sheet
* nonstick cooking spray
* 1 small apple

* 3 apple-sized onions
* 4 wooden caramel apple sticks
* 1 14-ounce (400-gram) package of caramels, unwrapped

* small cooking pot
* 1 tablespoon (15 mL) water
* spoon

This practical joke really brings on the tears because these caramel "apples" are made with onions!

Step 1: Lay a long piece of wax paper over a cookie sheet. Spray the paper with nonstick cooking spray.

Step 2: Wash and dry the apple. Then pull off the stem.

Step 3: Remove the papery outer layers of the onions.

Step 4: Push a wooden stick into one end of each onion. Also push a stick into the stem hole of the apple.

Step 5: Dump the caramels into a small cooking pot. Add the water. Melt the candy over low heat, stirring it with a spoon until it's smooth.

Step 6: Dip the apple in the hot caramel sauce, covering it completely. Place it on the wax paper. This one is for you!

Step 7: Dip the onions in the hot caramel sauce until they also are completely covered. Place them on the wax paper, slightly away from your apple.

Step 8: Place the cookie sheet in the refrigerator for one hour to cool the caramel.

Step 9: Invite your friends over for a tasty treat. Set the cookie sheet on the counter 15 minutes before they arrive, so the caramel softens.

Step 10: Before handing out the onions, take a bite of your apple. Make sure your friends see that it really is an apple. When they chomp into their onions, you'll get a good laugh from seeing their sour faces!

PSST! HERE'S THE POOP!

What You Need

* ¼ cup (60 mL) creamy peanut butter
* microwavable bowl
* chocolate syrup
* spoon

If you have a kid brother who is potty training, this practical joke will get your mom hopping mad! Just be sure to confess your joke so your brother doesn't get in trouble. And don't pout if your mom makes you clean up the mess. It will be worth it!

Step 1: Put the peanut butter in a microwavable bowl.

Step 2: Squirt a little chocolate syrup in the bowl. Use the spoon to mix it into the peanut butter. Keep adding chocolate syrup until it becomes as dark as you want it to look.

Step 3: Put the bowl in the microwave and set the timer to 10 seconds on high. This should make the mixture thinner.

Step 4: Let the peanut butter cool for 1 minute.

Step 5: Wipe the "poop" across the seat of the toilet. Then act disgusted as you call your mom in to see the "gift" your little brother left behind!

GAG·O·BARF·O·RAMA

What You Need

* small kitchen sponge
* small bowl
* red and green food coloring
* latex gloves
* 4-fluid ounce (118-mL) bottle of white craft glue
* wax paper
* scissors

Fake vomit is just as good at grossing people out as fake poop. This gag will make people gag!

Step 1: Tear the sponge into little pieces. Drop the pieces into the bowl and dribble drops of red and green food coloring over them.

Step 2: Put on the latex gloves. Use your fingers to mix the colors into the pieces. Then pour the glue over them. Use your fingers to evenly coat the sponge pieces.

Step 3: Pour the mixture onto a sheet of wax paper. Let it dry for three days.

Step 4: When it's hard, peel the fake vomit off the wax paper. Trim any jagged edges with a scissors.

Step 5: Place the fake vomit wherever it will get you the biggest reaction.

Pranks, Tricks, and Practical Jokes

SCARED YA!

What You Need

* ¼ cup (60 mL) water
* ¾ cup (175 mL) light corn syrup
* small bowl

* mixing spoon
* red food coloring
* chocolate syrup

Who says you have to save fake blood for Halloween? With this trick you can get a good scare from victims any time of the year.

Step 1: Mix water and corn syrup in the bowl.

Step 2: Stir in drops of food coloring. Keep adding drops until the shade is as red as real blood.

Step 3: Stir in drops of chocolate syrup a little bit at a time. The brown color will make your fake blood look real. Don't add too much syrup or the mixture will get too runny.

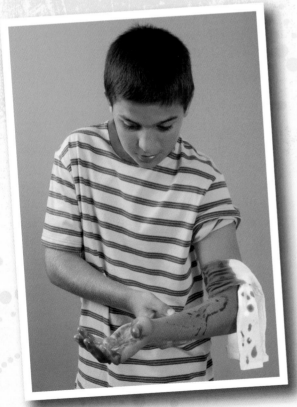

Step 4: Let the mixture sit in the bowl for 10 minutes. While you wait, put on some old clothes because the mixture might stain your clothing.

Step 5: Smear the fake blood on your face, neck, or body. Then go find a victim to scare!

IT'S A GUSHER!

What You Need

★ large pitcher ★ water ★ bathroom close to a group of people

This bathroom trick is a nifty way to embarrass your parents. Consider it a "must do" at their next big party.

Step 1: When no one is around, fill the pitcher with water.

Step 2: Hide the pitcher in the bathroom.

Step 3: When a crowd is standing near the bathroom, politely announce that you need to use the bathroom.

Step 4: Close the door behind you. Then pour your hidden water into the toilet as slowly as possible.

Step 5: Flush the toilet and walk out. As you pass by the crowd, say, "Man, I sure am thirsty!"

PEE YEEEWW!

What You Need

* small cup
* water
* yellow food coloring

Do your brothers and sisters get up in the middle of the night to pee? Then this practical joke is perfect! You could save it for a sleepover, but you probably won't be invited back!

Step 1: Fill the cup half full with water.

Step 2: Add drops of food coloring to the water until it looks like pee.

Step 3: Use your fingers to flick drops of the fake pee on the open toilet seat and on the floor all around the toilet.

If your victim doesn't step or sit in the fake pee, he or she will certainly see it. Be prepared for shouts of, "Eew, gross!"

SECRET LETTERS

What You Need

* fresh lemon
* knife
* small bowl
* fine-tip paintbrush
* white paper
* blow dryer

You need to get a top secret message to a friend, but how? Start squeezing. With just a lemon, your privacy is a slam dunk.

Step 1: Carefully cut a lemon into wedges with a knife. Squeeze the juice from each wedge into the bowl.

Step 2: Dip the paintbrush into the lemon juice. Wipe large drops of juice against the side of the bowl.

Step 3: Write your message on a sheet of white paper. Let the juice dry.

Step 4: Then pass the piece of paper to your friend. Tell him to heat the paper with a blow dryer. The acid in the lemon juice turns brown when heated. Your message will magically appear.

IT'S ALL IN THE FOLD

What You Need

* ★ dollar bill
* ★ 2 small paper clips

This trick is simple, yet it's impressive for anyone who sees it for the first time. You fold a dollar bill together with loose paper clips. But when you unfold the bill, the paper clips are "magically" linked together.

2 & 3

Step 1: When you have an audience, grab your dollar bill and two paper clips.

Step 2: Fold the left end of the bill about a third of the way to the right edge.

Step 3: Paper clip the two layers of the bill together along its top edge. The paper clip should be centered on the folded portion.

Step 4: Fold the right end of the bill behind and toward the left edge. Push the end a little past the edge.

4 & 5

Step 5: As you did in step 3, paper clip the two new layers of the bill together along the top edge. The front of the second paper clip slips through the folded loop on the left.

Step 6: Show your audience the front and back of the bill. They will see one clip on one side of the bill. The second clip will be on the other side of the bill.

Step 7: Now grasp the two ends of the bill and pull it apart hard. Say, "Watch as the two paper clips magically link together!"

Step 8: After the paper clips fly off, pick them up to show the audience they are indeed joined.

DIVE-BOMBING EGG

What You Need

* hard-boiled egg
* 16-fluid ounce (473 mL) glass juice bottle

* 4 matches and a matchbook

Ever seen a boiled egg shrink and squeeze into an opening smaller than itself? Neither have your friends—until now.

Step 1: Peel the hard-boiled egg.

Step 2: Stand an empty glass juice bottle on a table.

Step 3: Set the egg upright on the mouth of the bottle. Show your friends that there is no way the egg will fit through the mouth of the bottle. Then remove the egg.

Step 4: Hold four matches together by their bottom ends. Light them all at once. Ask an adult to do this part if you don't like to use matches.

Step 5: Hold the lit matches over the mouth of the bottle for a few seconds. Give them time to burn down a little.

Step 6: Drop the matches into the bottom of the bottle. Quickly balance one end of the egg on the bottle like you did in step 3.

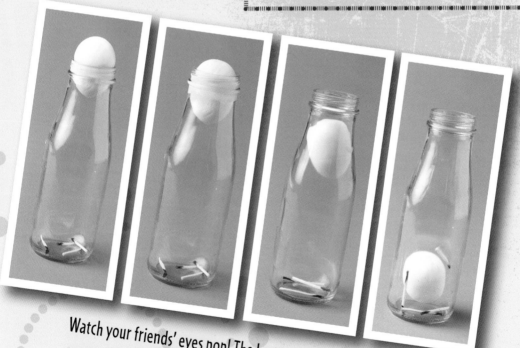

Watch your friends' eyes pop! The heat of the matches will slowly squeeze the egg and suck it into the bottle! The egg will return to its normal shape after it drops into the bottle.

Pranks, Tricks, and Practical Jokes

79

JUMPING ACES

What You Need

* ★ four aces from a deck of cards

This magic card trick is easy to master in seconds. But the audience may never figure out how you're pulling the wool over their eyes.

Step 1: Pull the four aces from a deck of cards. Set the rest of the deck aside.

Step 2: Fan the four cards toward your audience so they see the four aces.

Step 3: Put the cards back to back, so that a red ace and a black ace are in each hand.

Step 4: Hold the pairs out to your audience so that both black aces are facing them.

Step 5: Bring the aces close together in your hands so the black aces face each other. The red aces will face your palms.

Step 6: Wrap your fingers around the side of the cards closest to your audience. This hides that you're holding the cards in your left hand by your right middle finger and right thumb. Likewise, the right-hand cards are held by your left middle finger and left thumb.

Step 7: Bring the cards up to your lips and blow hard on them as you pull your hands down and apart. The blowing is to cover up that you're pulling the cards in your left hand down with your right fingers. This makes the red ace in your left hand face the outside.

Step 8: Show the audience that the red aces are now facing them. They'll be amazed!

Step 9: Blow on the cards again and flip the aces back to black. The secret to mastering this trick is to move your hands so quickly that the audience doesn't catch on.

Know IT

What do military vehicles, aliens, monster trucks, mummies, and robots have in common? They are all really cool and you want to know more about them. So turn the pages, and let's get started!

GUNSLINGER

JE PRO NEAL
OLIVER

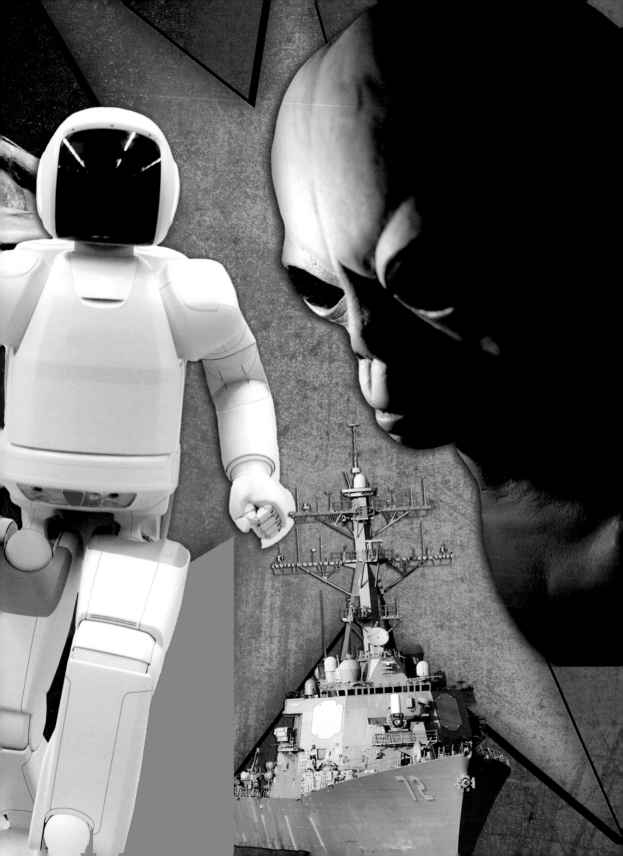

TANKS AND M VEHICLES

Military machines have important missions. It's the tank's job to search for and destroy enemies. The military uses these big bullies to strike fear into the enemy. They also keep crews safe with their heavy armor. Three Abrams tank variations are in use today. They are the M1, M1A1, and M1A2. Soldiers call the Abrams "The Beast" and "Dracula."

M1A1 ABRAMS

The M2 machine gun takes out targets with light armor.

The 120-millimeter main gun launches a variety of rounds. The range is about 2 miles (3.2 kilometers).

The track runs on seven road wheels on each side. The track is about 2 feet (61 centimeters) wide.

THE CREW

The Abrams has a crew of four. The tank commander directs the mission. The driver steers the tank. The gunner finds targets and fires the main gun and two machine guns. The loader keeps weapons loaded and fires another machine gun.

Crew members can sit in the turret. The main gun is also mounted on the turret.

The drive wheel on each side is powered by the engine. The drive wheel moves the whole track.

85

SHIPS

When a military response is needed, the president asks, "Where are the carriers?" Carriers are like small cities. They even have their own zip codes. About 2,500 airmen join the other 3,000 sailors aboard. It's like having a city that can move around the world and respond to any threat, anywhere.

The catapults on aircraft carriers propel airplanes to 165 miles (265 kilometers) per hour in two seconds! A carrier has four catapults.

The hull is made from steel plates several inches thick.

The hangar deck is below the flight deck. More than 80 aircraft are stored here.

The engine rooms contain nuclear-powered engine systems. They produce more than 280,000 horsepower.

The island houses the bridge and primary flight control—pri-fly. The captain directs the carrier's actions and movements from the bridge. The Air Boss directs the aircraft from pri-fly.

The top deck is the flight deck. Planes take off and land here for a fast air strike.

The arresting gear lands a plane in just two seconds. A plane's tailhook grabs a wire stretched across the landing strip. The wire connects to an engine that absorbs the force of the plane as it lands.

Elevators move aircraft from the hangar deck to the flight deck.

UNMANNED VEHICLES

To keep troops out of harm's way, the military is experimenting with vehicles without people inside. The vehicles can explode mines, watch enemy movement, and launch missiles. Meanwhile, the crew operates them by remote from miles away. In the future you can expect more use of robots in the armed forces.

Pack bot is designed to fit in a soldier's backpack. Soldiers can control its arm remotely to explode bombs and other weapons.

MQ-1B Predator

The MQ-1 Predator and MQ-9 Reaper are about the size of small passenger planes. They gather information on the enemy. They also carry and launch missiles.

The Gladiator looks like a mini tank. It can be mounted with cameras and guns. It also can shoot grenades.

The Raven weighs less than 5 pounds (2.3 kilograms) and can be launched by hand. It gathers information on the enemy.

TYPES OF ALIENS

People who claim to have been abducted by aliens tend to have similar stories. A few kinds of aliens are mentioned over and over again. The aliens fall into four main groups.

Grays

Most reports of alien abductions describe aliens known as Grays or Greys. They get their name from their skin color. Most Grays are less than 5 feet (150 centimeters) tall. They have large bald heads and big black eyes. Grays are said to experiment on humans.

Reptilians

Reptilians might be best described as giant lizards standing upright like a person. They have scaly green skin and long arms and legs. Reptilians are never described as nice. Witnesses say they are violent and mean. They think of humans as lesser beings.

Nordics

Nordics look like many people from Nordic countries, such as Sweden or Norway. They are tall, blond, and fair-skinned. They have very large blue eyes. Nordics are not usually described as mean and don't usually abduct people.

Hybrids

Some alien abductees say they have seen human-alien hybrids. These hybrids are usually a cross between a human and a Gray. Abductees claim that Grays do experiments on humans to create these hybrid aliens.

MYSTERY IN ROSWELL

The Roswell UFO event is probably the most well-known UFO sighting in history. It all began in early July 1947.

William "Mack" Brazel was working on a farm near Roswell, New Mexico. He discovered broken pieces of shiny metal scattered over one of the fields. A few days later, Brazel told the Roswell sheriff about the site. The sheriff called officials at the U.S. military base in Roswell.

A Second Site

On July 4, at a site nearby, Jim Ragsdale said a UFO crashed into the side of a cliff. Ragsdale saw alien bodies. He said the aliens were very short, with large heads and eyes. Their skin was a pale gray color. He said he left when he saw military vehicles arriving at the site.

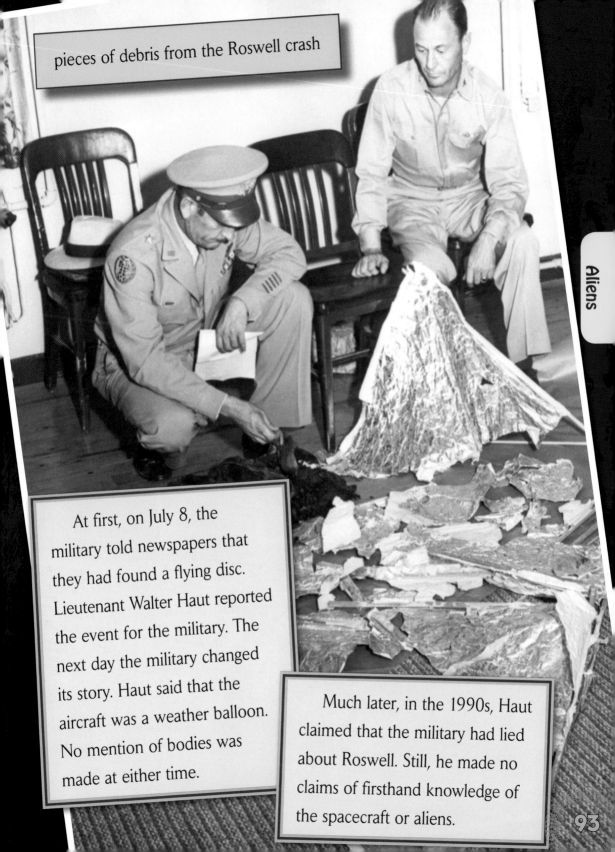

pieces of debris from the Roswell crash

At first, on July 8, the military told newspapers that they had found a flying disc. Lieutenant Walter Haut reported the event for the military. The next day the military changed its story. Haut said that the aircraft was a weather balloon. No mention of bodies was made at either time.

Much later, in the 1990s, Haut claimed that the military had lied about Roswell. Still, he made no claims of firsthand knowledge of the spacecraft or aliens.

Top Secret Project?

In 1995 the Air Force published a report on the events at Roswell. They said a top secret project, called MOGUL, was responsible for the Roswell debris. The military had been testing an electronic device to listen for Soviet bomb testing. The large metal device was attached to a special weather balloon. At the time military officials had called the Roswell craft an ordinary weather balloon to cover up its top secret status.

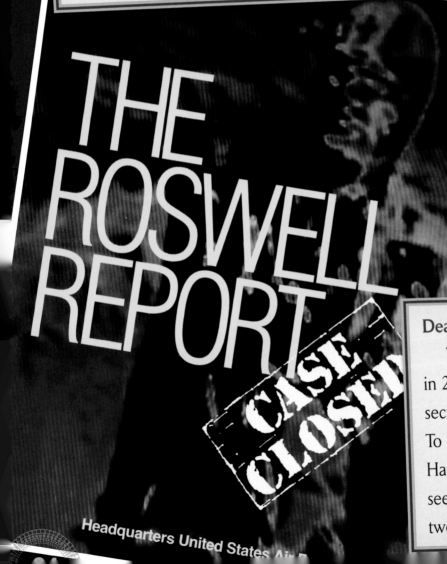

THE ROSWELL REPORT

CASE CLOSED

Headquarters United States Air

Deathbed Statement

When Walter Haut d
in 2005, he left behind
secret written statement
To everyone's surprise,
Haut wrote that he had
seen the spaceship and
two alien bodies himsel

Over the years witness accounts have been questioned. Jim Ragsdale's story changed. He said that he took the aliens' helmets. He then buried the helmets but forgot the location. Concerns have been raised about Haut's memory in his last years, when his secret statement was written.

Walter Haut (left) in 1997

Countless books and TV shows have been done on Roswell. Thousands of people attend the UFO festival there every year. The Roswell incident will likely remain a mystery for years to come.

MONSTER TRUCK STANDOUTS

Monster truck designers are nothing if not creative. They've built many crazy and unique trucks, including these standouts.

The Black Stallion has been around since the early monster truck days. Mike Vaters added 40-inch (102-centimeter) tires to his street-driven Ford. Today Stallion runs on 66-inch (168-centimeter) tires. Vaters is a seven-time Thunder Nationals champion.

The original Grave Digger was built from a 1951 Ford pickup chassis. It had a Chevy engine and lots of spare parts. In 1986 the truck received its graveyard paint job. Former owner and current driver Dennis Anderson is known for wild driving and super stunts. Grave Digger is one of the most popular monster trucks of all time.

MONSTER CREATIONS

Some machines in the monster truck world aren't trucks at all. Monster truck creators are limited only by their imaginations.

How do you get more monster than a monster truck? You build a monster tank. Popular in the late 1980s, monster tanks included Heavy Metal, Nitecrawler, and Bigfoot Fastrax. At 20,000 pounds (9,000 kilograms), they were twice the weight of a monster truck.

Monster Jerky is a unique monster. Its designer, Frank Schettini, was a dirt bike racer. He made a monster truck that was part dirt bike. To drive, Frank stands in a harness. He steers with handlebars and controls speed and braking with hand controls. It's hard for other drivers to control, but for Frank it comes naturally.

ROBOSAURUS

Robosaurus eats monster trucks for breakfast. This giant 40-foot- (12-meter-) tall robot has 1-foot (30-centimeter) teeth. Robosaurus breathes fire too. A driver strapped inside the head controls the beast.

Ice Mummies

Snow, ice, and cold temperatures can keep bodies frozen in time. Like the heat of the desert, extreme cold kills bacteria. Without bacteria to eat flesh, a dead body can become a natural mummy.

OTZI, THE ICEMAN

In 1991 mountain climbers found a frozen mummy in the Otzal Alps in Italy. He was nicknamed "Otzi" for the mountains where he was found. Researchers believe Otzi died about 5,300 years ago from an arrow wound in his shoulder.

Otzi has 57 tattoos. Researchers think he made them by using a needle to inject fireplace soot under his skin. The tattoos may have served as pain relief rather than decoration. Today some people relieve pain with acupuncture. This treatment involves sticking needles into pressure points in the skin.

JUANITA, THE ICE MAIDEN

In 1995 scientist Johan Reinhard was exploring the Andes Mountains in Peru. He discovered the mummy of an Inca girl preserved in ice. Reinhard named the mummy Juanita, but most people know her as the Ice Maiden. Scientists believe she died about 500 years ago from a blow to the back of her head.

The Ice Maiden was probably sacrificed to the gods. The Inca believed that human sacrifice pleased the gods. The gods would then protect the rest of the community from harm.

Fun Fact:

Food companies use a process similar to ice mummification to produce lightweight items with long shelf lives. Freeze-dried foods include instant coffee and meal pouches for campers and soldiers.

Bog Mummies

Heat and cold aren't the only things that create natural mummies. Many mummies have been found in the swampy peat bogs of northern Europe. The cold, acidic bog water preserves flesh, turning it to a leathery texture. These mummies are known as bog people.

CRIMINALS OR SACRIFICES?

The bog people were Germans and Celts who lived about 2,000 years ago. Many of the bog mummies appear to have been killed violently. Some had smashed skulls or cut throats. Others had nooses around their necks or were tied to heavy rocks.

Scientists believe that people accused of some crimes were killed and dumped in the bogs. Others may have been sacrificed to the gods.

Fun Fact:

Tollund Man is probably the most famous bog mummy. He was found in Tollund, Denmark, in 1950. The well-preserved mummy still has the stubble on his chin!

Everyone knows about Egyptian mummies. But other cultures also preserved their dead. The Egyptians weren't even the first to do it.

CHILEAN MUMMIES

Thousands of years before the pharaohs, the Chinchorros of northern Chile made mummies. Beginning in about 5000 BC, they rebuilt their dead. They first removed the skin and internal organs. Next they dried the bones and attached them to twigs for reinforcement. Over this framework, they reattached the skin. They then applied a thick layer of ash paste over the body. Next they coated the body with red ocher or a metal called manganese. A clay mask covered the face, and some wore wigs of human hair. The Chinchorros may have honored the mummies by displaying them at feasts and festivals.

MUMMY BUNDLES OF PERU

About 500 years ago Inca people in Peru mummified their dead in a sitting position. They wrapped them in layers of cloth to create bundles. Each layer contained items that the dead person might need in the afterlife, such as weapons and plates. Some of these mummy bundles weigh more than 200 pounds (91 kilograms).

MYSTERY MUMMIES OF CHINA

Beginning in the late 1970s, natural mummies with light brown, red, and blond hair were found in the Tarim Basin of western China. Scientists were surprised that these desert mummies looked European instead of Asian.

Researchers studied the clothes of the mummies for answers. Cherchen Man is a 6-foot 6-inch (198-centimeter) mummy who died around 1000 BC. He wore woolen leggings in a plaid pattern similar to those worn by men in Scotland. From this clue, some historians believe that he was a Celt. These people lived in Europe from around 800 BC until AD 400. Most settled in the British Isles. But they may have come from central Asia sometime after 3000 BC and split into two groups. One group may have headed west toward Europe and the other east toward China.

ROBOT EXPLORERS

Robots are a very real part of our world, and they're out of this world! Space is cold and people can't breathe up there. Humans need a lot of equipment to survive in space. Robots don't have the same problems. They help scientists explore the mysteries of other worlds.

ROBONAUT

NASA is developing Robonaut to help astronauts with daily tasks. This robot has a head, body, arms, and hands with fingers that bend. Robonauts could hand tools to astronauts and prepare work sites. They'll help clean up after the astronauts too.

Exploring Mars

In 2004 two robot rovers, Spirit and Opportunity, landed on Mars. Scientists planned for these rovers to explore the planet for 90 days. Years later they were still at it, although Spirit got stuck in sand in 2010.

The robots use their arms to scrape and chip rock samples. Both robots have cameras to take pictures of Mars' surface. The Mars rovers sometimes run on their own. A person on Earth sends the robot a message telling it a location to reach. The rovers use their sensors to decide the best path to get there.

Fun Fact:

Spirit and Opportunity found proof that liquid water once flowed on Mars.

Ocean Explorers

You don't need to go to space to find danger. Two-thirds of Earth's surface is covered by water. Most of this area remains unexplored, especially the deep sea. Robot explorers are built to withstand the very high pressure and cold temperatures of the deep sea.

ROVs

Remotely Operated Vehicles (ROVs) can dive to the deepest parts of the ocean. They are controlled remotely. A cable connects them to a power source on a surface ship. ROVs are used for exploring sunken ships, repairing the walls of dams, and fixing oil rigs.

Fun Fact:

There are more than 3,000 ROVs in use throughout the world.

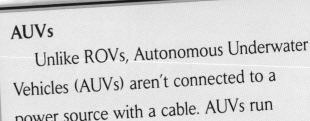

AUVs

Unlike ROVs, Autonomous Underwater Vehicles (AUVs) aren't connected to a power source with a cable. AUVs run on batteries. They are programmed for a mission and carry it out. They are often used to map the seafloor.

A MINE-HUNTING CRAB

A six-legged military robot is being designed to find and explode mines on shorelines. Like a crab, Ariel can move forward, backward, and sideways.

FUTURE ROBOTS

In the future robots will likely be a large part of people's everyday lives. Some robots will be almost human in how they look and act. If you can imagine it, scientists are probably working on it right now. Future robots are closer than you think.

Self-Driving Cars

Scientists are making strides in the quest for a self-driving car. The Grand Challenge was a contest for autonomous vehicles. Using sensors and global positioning systems, vehicles had to drive themselves through a desert obstacle course. No vehicles finished the first contest in 2004. But in 2005 a team from Stanford University completed and won the challenge.

The 2007 Urban Challenge course was meant to copy city driving. Tartan Racing, a team including Carnegie Mellon University, General Motors, and others, won the race.

Grand Challenge race

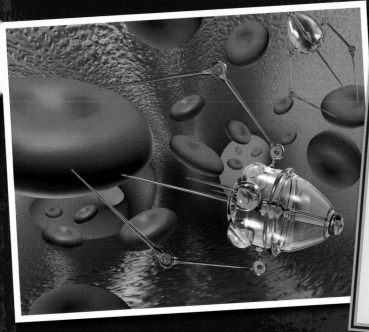

Nanobots

A nanobot is a robot so small you would need a microscope to see it. Imagine robots like these traveling to a diseased human cell. It would be able to destroy the cell without hurting the healthy cells around it.

Cyborgs

What would you do with the strength of 100 men? How about the eyesight of an eagle? Future robots might be a combination of human and robot parts, called a cyborg. A human brain could run a robot body. Or a human could have special robotic arms or legs. Although robotic arms and legs are under study, most scientists think true cyborgs are far in the future.

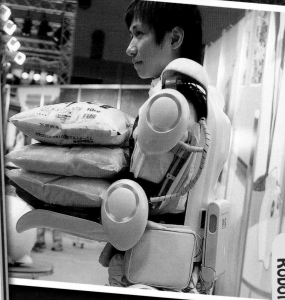

Capstone Press,
151 Good Counsel Drive, P.O. Box 669,
Mankato, MN 56002
www.capstonepub.com

 Books published by Capstone Press are manufactured with paper containing
at least 10 percent post-consumer waste.

Library of Congress Cataloging-in-Publication Data
The ultimate kids' guide to fun : experiments, projects, games and knowledge
    every kid should know / by Barbara H. Davis ... [et al.].
    p. cm.—(Edge books. Kids' guides)
  ISBN 978-1-4296-6638-1 (paperback)
  1. Amusements—Juvenile literature. 2. Recreation—Juvenile literature.
    3. Games—Juvenile literature. I. Davis, Barbara H,. II. Title. III. Series.
GV182.9.U65 2011
790.1922—dc22   2011004951

Editorial Credits

Chris Harbo, Angie Kaelberer, and Mandy Robbins, editors; Kyle Grenz and Gene
Bentdahl, designers; Eric Manske, production specialist; Marcy Morin, scheduler

Photo Credits

Alamy Images: Eye Ubiquitous, 104, John T. Fowler, 103, Robert Harding Picture Library Ltd., 102, 105;
AlienUFOart.com: William L. McDonald, 91 (middle and bottom); American Honda Motor Co., Inc.: cover
(robot), 3 (robot), 83 (left); AP Images: Air Force, 94; Art Life Images: Bigfoot 4x4, Inc., 98, Dave & Bev
Huntoon, 96, 97; Capstone Press/TJ Thoraldson Digital Photography: cover (paper airplane), 3 (apple, paper
airplane and kids), 6, 8, 9, 10, 11, 12, 13, 14, 15, 16, 17, 18 (left), 19, 20, 21, 22, 23, 24, 25, 26, 27, 28, 29, 30, 31, 38
(top), 39, 44, 45, 47, 48, 49, 50, 51, 52, 53, 54, 55, 56, 57, 58, 59, 60, 61, 62 (left), 64, 65 (top), 66, 67 (top left and
right), 68, 69, 70, 71(top left and right, bottom left and middle), 72, 76, 77, 78, 79, 80, 81; Capstone Studio/Karon
Dubke: 3 (balloons and birdfeeder), 7 (balloons and birdfeeder), 18 (right), 32, 33, 34, 35, 36, 37, 71 (bottom
right), 75; Corbis: Bettmann, 93, Sygma/Vienna Report Agency, 100; Defenseimagery.mil: LCPL Patrick Green,
USMC, 89 (middle), Tech. Sgt. Sabrina Johnson, 89 (top); Department of Defense: DARPA, 110; Ed Shems: 3
(illustration), 38 (bottom), 62 (right), 63, 65 (bottom), 67 (bottom), 73, 74; Fortean Picture Library: 92, 95; Getty
Images, Inc.: AFP/Major Fromentin, 108, Koichi Kamoshida, 111 (bottom); iStockphoto: Jared DeCinque, cover
(tank), LindaMarieB, 91 (top); Mary Evans Picture Library, 90 (bottom); NASA: 106, Jet Propulsion Laboratory,
107; Newscom: AFP/Getty Images, 101; Photo Researchers, Inc.: Peter Menzel, 109 (bottom); Shutterstock: Felix
Mizioznikov, 82 (bottom), Fotocrisis, 111 (top), Peter Albrektsen, cover (truck), photoBeard, 3 (alien), 83 (right),
Shiva, 90 (top), Studio 37, 82 (top); unlimitedcustoms.com: 99 (top); U.S. Air Force: Master Sgt. Andy Dunaway,
cover (F-16 plane), Senior Airman Julianne Showalter, 89 (bottom); U.S. Army: Spc. Luke Thornberry, 85 (inset);
U.S. Navy: Illustration courtesy Northrop Grumman Newport News Shipbuilding, 86-87, MC1 David McKee,
88, MC2 Jason R. Zalasky, 3 (ship), 7 (middle), PH1 Ted Banks, 84-85; Woods Hole Oceanographic Institution:
Chris Linder, 109 (top); www.robosaurus.com: 99 (bottom)

Printed in the United States of America in Stevens Point, Wisconsin.

062011   006229F11